Contents

Foreword by

The Prime Minister, Tony Blair

The Government has a mission to modernise – renewing our country for the new millennium. We are modernising our schools, our hospitals, our economy and our criminal justice system. We are modernising our democratic framework, with new arrangements for Scotland, Wales, Northern Ireland, the English regions, Parliament and local authorities.

But modernisation must go further. It must engage with how government itself works. Modernising government is a vital part of our programme of renewal for Britain. The old arguments about government are now outdated – big government against small government, interventionism against laissez-faire. The new issues are the right issues: modernising government, better government, getting government right.

Modernising Government is a significant step forward in what is a long-term programme of reform. It puts in place a number of important initiatives, and sets out an agenda for the future. But in line with the Government's overall modernisation programme, in line with our policy of investment for reform, it is modernisation for a purpose: modernising government to get better government – for a better Britain.

Introduction by the
Minister for the Cabinet Office,

Jack Cunningham

Modernising Government is an important statement for the Government. It is a programme of reform for the future. And it is a series of new measures which the Government will implement now.

But Modernising Government is also about something else. It is a clear statement by the Government of what government is for. Not government for those who work in government; but government for people – people as consumers, people as citizens.

That doesn't mean to say that those whose job it is to deliver public services are not important. Far from it; they are central. For too long, they have been denigrated. This Government values public servants, and public services – and we will continue to do so.

But in doing so, we will make sure that government services are better – that they reflect real lives and deliver what people really want. Better provision of better services available from government at all levels is central to the approach of Modernising Government – in schools, in hospitals, in doctors' surgeries, in police stations, in benefit offices, in Jobcentres, in local councils. To improve the way we provide services, we need all parts of government to work together better. We need joined-up government. We need integrated government. And we need to make sure that government services are brought forward using the best and most modern techniques, to match the best of the private sector – including one-stop shops, single contacts which link in to a range of government Departments and especially electronic information-age services.

These are key new initiatives. It is important that we act upon them now – and we will. But modernising government is a long-term programme. Modernising Government is a key step forward in that programme, and a road-map for its future. It sets out a challenge for all of us in government: a challenge to modernise government, to create better government to make life better for people.

Jack Cunningham.

Executive summary

Modernising government is central to the Government's programme of renewal and reform.

In line with the Government's overall programme of modernisation, Modernising Government is **modernisation for a purpose – to make life better for people and businesses.**

Modernising Government is a **long-term programme of improvement**.

But the Government is putting forward a **new package of reforms** now:

- A commitment to ensure that public services are available **24 hours a day, seven days a week** where there is a demand, for example **by the end of 2000** everyone being able to phone **NHS Direct at any time** for healthcare advice.

- **Joined-up government in action** – including a clear commitment for people to be able to notify different parts of government of details such as a change of address **simply and electronically in one transaction.**

- **A new drive to remove unnecessary regulation**, and a requirement on Departments preparing policies which impose new regulatory burdens to submit high quality **Regulatory Impact Assessments** and to consult the Cabinet Office in advance.

- A **new target** of all dealings with government being **deliverable electronically by 2008.**

- New '**Learning Labs**' to encourage new ways of front-line working **by suspending rules that stifle innovation.**

- Taking a more creative approach to financial and other **incentives** for public service staff, including a commitment to explore the scope for **financial reward** for staff who identify financial savings or service improvements.

- Within Whitehall, **a new focus on delivery** - asking every Permanent Secretary to ensure that their Department has the capacity to drive through achievement of the key government targets and to take a personal responsibility for ensuring that this happens. Bringing **more people in from outside** and bringing able, younger people up the ladder more quickly.

To ensure that government is both inclusive and integrated, we have **three aims in modernising government**:

- Ensuring that policy making is more **joined up and strategic.**

- Making sure that **public service users**, not providers, are the focus, by matching services more closely to people's lives.

- Delivering public services that are **high quality and efficient.**

We are centring our programme on **five key commitments**:

- **Policy making**: we will be **forward looking** in developing policies to deliver outcomes that matter, not simply reacting to short-term pressures. We will:

  - identify and spread best practice through the new Centre for Management and Policy Studies.

  - bring in joint training of Ministers and civil servants.

  - introduce peer review of Departments.

- **Responsive public services**: we will deliver public services to **meet the needs of citizens**, not the convenience of service providers. We will:

  - deliver a big push on obstacles to joined-up working, through local partnerships, one-stop shops, and other means.

  - involve and meet the needs of all different groups in society.

- **Quality public services**: we will deliver efficient, high quality public services and **will not tolerate mediocrity**. We will:

  - review all central and local government department services and activities over the next five years to identify the best supplier in each case.

  - set new targets for all public bodies, focusing on real improvements in the quality and effectiveness of public services.

  - monitor performance closely so that we strike the right balance between intervening where services are failing and giving successful organisations the freedom to manage.

- **Information age government**: we will use **new technology** to meet the needs of citizens and business, and not trail behind technological developments. We will:

  - develop an IT strategy for Government which will establish cross-government co-ordination machinery and frameworks on such issues as use of digital signatures and smart cards, websites and call centres.

  - benchmark progress against targets for electronic services.

- **Public service**: we will **value public service**, not denigrate it. We will:

  - modernise the civil service, revise performance management arrangements, tackle under-representation of women, ethnic minorities and people with disabilities and build the capability for innovation.

  - establish a public sector employment forum to bring together and develop key players across the public sector.

This long-term programme of **modernisation for a purpose** will move us towards our central objective in modernising government:

Better government to make life better for people.

Marks projects and initiatives where further information is available on the internet. The websites addresses are listed in the Appendix on pages 64,65,66

1. Vision

1. Vision

1. Government matters. We all want it to deliver policies, programmes and services that will make us more healthy, more secure and better equipped to tackle the challenges we face. Government should improve the quality of our lives.

2. Modernisation is vital if government is to achieve that ambition. Government must face the challenge of the times, and embrace the opportunity it offers:

- We live in an age when most of the old dogmas that haunted governments in the past have been swept away. We know now that better government is about much more than whether public spending should go up or down, or whether organisations should be nationalised or privatised. Now that we are not hidebound by the old ways of government we can find new and better ones.

- Information technology is revolutionising our lives, including the way we work, the way we communicate and the way we learn. The information age offers huge scope for organising government activities in new, innovative and better ways and for making life easier for the public by providing public services in integrated, imaginative and more convenient forms like single gateways, the Internet and digital TV.

- We must unleash the potential within the public service to drive our modernising agenda right across government. There is great enthusiasm and determination within the public service to tackle the problems which face society, to do the job better.

- Distinctions between services delivered by the public and the private sector are breaking down in many areas, opening the way to new ideas, partnerships and opportunities for devising and delivering what the public wants.

3. Modernisation is a hallmark of the Government. We are rebuilding the National Health Service. We are raising standards in education. We are modernising our constitution and local government. We are reforming our welfare system so that it will truly and fairly address the needs of our society. We are tackling crime in new ways. We are modernising our defence capability and Armed Forces. We have a new, positive relationship with our partners in Europe.

4. But modernisation must not stop there. To achieve these goals we must modernise the way government itself works:

- The way we devise our policies and programmes.

- The way we deliver services to individual citizens and businesses.

- The way we perform all the other functions of a modern government.

5. Modernisation, though, must be for a purpose: to create better government to make life better for people. Just as the Government is pursuing the aims of investment for reform and money for modernisation in the way it decides on spending programmes, so too must modernisation of government be a means to achieving better government – better policy making, better responsiveness to what people want, better public services.

6. People want government which meets their needs, which is available when they need it, and which delivers results for them. People want effective government, both where it responds directly to their needs – such as in healthcare, education and the social services – and where it acts for society as a whole, such as protecting the environment, promoting public health and maintaining our prison and immigration services and defence capability.

7. To achieve that, the Government's strategy is one in which the keystones of its operations are inclusiveness and integration:

- **Inclusive:** policies are forward looking, inclusive and fair.

- **Integrated:** policies and programmes, local and national, tackle the issues facing society – like crime, drugs, housing and the environment – in a joined up way, regardless of the organisational structure of government.

8. The Government is putting these principles into practice by aiming to:

- provide public services of the highest quality, matching the best anywhere in the world in their ability to innovate, share good ideas, control costs and above all to deliver what they are supposed to.

- ensure that government is responsive to the user and is, from the public's point of view, seamless.

- make certain that citizens and business will have choice about how and when to access government services – whether from home via interactive TV, via call centres, via one-stop shops or, indeed, post offices, libraries, banks or supermarkets.

9. People are exercising choice and demanding higher quality. In the private sector, service standards and service delivery have improved as a result. People are now rightly demanding a better service not just from the private sector, but from the public sector too.

10. The Government is committed to public service. But that does not mean public services should stand still. Public servants must be the agents of the changes citizens and businesses want. We will build on the many strengths in the public sector to equip it with a culture of improvement, innovation and collaborative purpose. Public sector staff need to respond to these challenges, working in partnership to deliver this programme.

London Borough of Enfield – Housing Management.

Peterborough City Council – Building Control Services.

11. Some parts of the public service are as efficient, dynamic and effective as anything in the private sector. But other parts are not. There are numerous reasons for this, and some are common to many governments around the world:

- **Organisation:** because institutions tend to look after their own interests, public services can be organized too much around the structure of the providers rather than the users. This can be evident in their opening hours, their locations, the demands they make of citizens; the help they do and do not provide when they are needed; and the extent to which they link up with other service providers to offer services in packages that are relevant to people's lives.

- **Inertia:** although the public can express its dissatisfaction with its public service through the ballot box, this can be a blunt instrument, removing whole local or central governments intermittently and often not addressing the underlying reasons why things are wrong. The risk is that particular parts of the public sector can therefore be left to fail for too long.

- **Inputs not outcomes:** the system in Whitehall and elsewhere – in particular the importance attached traditionally to the annual spending negotiations – has meant that Ministers, Departments and units have often been forced to devote much of their effort to maximising their funding rather than considering what difference they can make in the form of actual results or outcomes.

- **Risk aversion:** the cultures of Parliament, Ministers and the civil service create a situation in which the rewards for success are limited and penalties for failure can be severe. The system is too often risk averse. As a result, Ministers and public servants can be slow to take advantage of new opportunities.

- **Management:** over the past 20 years, various management changes within the public service have improved value for money and quality in the way services are delivered by organisations. But too little attention has gone into making sure that policies, programmes and services across the board are devised and implemented in ways that best meet people's needs, where necessary by working across institutional boundaries.

- **Denigration:** public servants are hard-working and dedicated and many are as innovative and entrepreneurial as anyone outside government. But they have been wrongly denigrated and demoralised for too long. There has been a presumption that the private sector is always best, and insufficient attention has been given to rewarding success in the public service and to equipping it with the skills required to develop and deliver strategic policies and services in modern and effective ways.

12. To help counter some of these difficulties, the Government is working in partnership – partnership with the new, devolved ways of government in Scotland, Wales and Northern Ireland, and partnership with local authorities, other organisations, and other countries.

13. Devolution is a crucial part of the Government's modernisation programme. It is a stimulus to fresh thinking about the business of government. All parts of the United Kingdom stand to benefit from it. We are setting up three new devolved administrations in Scotland, Wales and Northern Ireland. We will also, in time, move towards elected regional assemblies in England. This White Paper sets out commitments on behalf of the Government of the United Kingdom. We hope the devolved administrations will join us in taking the programme forward. We want to co-operate with them in areas which straddle our respective responsibilities.

14. Local government is responsible for a quarter of public expenditure on services, including education, social services, police, housing and public transport. We have worked very closely with the Local Government Association and other bodies in preparing this White Paper. Local government must be an equal partner in our drive to modernise government. We want to encourage initiatives to establish partnerships in delivering services, by all parts of government in ways that fit local circumstances; and to establish common targets, financial frameworks, IT links, management controls and accountability mechanisms that support such arrangements. We will continue to involve other groups too, including business and the voluntary sector.

15. We will continue to work closely with the public sector trade unions to achieve our shared goals of committed, fair, efficient and effective public services.

16. There is no such thing as a 'typical' citizen. People's needs and concerns differ: between women and men for example, between the young and the old; and between those of different social, cultural and educational backgrounds and people with disabilities. Some of these concerns have not been given sufficient recognition in the past. We must understand the needs of all people and respond to them. This, too, is a crucial part of modernising government.

17. We are exchanging ideas with other countries on policy making, on delivering services and on using information technology in new and innovative ways. We are learning from each other.

18. Modernising government means identifying, and defeating, the problems we face. It means freeing the public service so that it can build on its strengths to innovate and to rise to these challenges. It means raising all standards until they match the best within and outside the public service, and continue improving. It means transforming government, so that it is organised around what the public wants and needs, rather than around the needs or convenience of institutions.

19. This White Paper sets out our programme for modernising government. It does not pretend to have all the answers. This is a large project and we live in a fast-moving world. The Government is therefore presenting an agenda for progress. We explain what we think the current problems and challenges are, where we have made a start in tackling them, and how we plan to take our work forward in the future.

20. We are centring our programme on five key commitments:

- **Policy making:** we will be forward looking in developing policies to deliver results that matter, not simply reacting to short-term pressures.

- **Responsive public services:** we will deliver public services to meet the needs of citizens, not the convenience of service providers.

- **Quality public services:** we will deliver efficient, high quality public services and will not tolerate mediocrity.

- **Information age government:** we will use new technology to meet the needs of citizens and business, and not trail behind technological developments

- **Public service:** we will value public service, not denigrate it.

2. Policy making

2. Policy making:

We will be forward looking in developing policies to deliver outcomes that matter, not simply reacting to short-term pressures

1. Policy making is the process by which governments translate their political vision into programmes and actions to deliver 'outcomes' – desired changes in the real world. Many of the other issues considered in this White Paper cannot be seen in isolation from the policy making process. Government cannot succeed in delivering the outcomes people want if the policies and programmes they are implementing are flawed or inadequate.

2. People are becoming more demanding, whether as consumers of goods and services in the market place, as citizens or as businesses affected by the policies and services which government provides. To meet these demands, government must be willing constantly to re-evaluate what it is doing so as to produce policies that really deal with problems; that are forward-looking and shaped by the evidence rather than a response to short-term pressures; that tackle causes not symptoms; that are measured by results rather than activity; that are flexible and innovative rather than closed and bureaucratic; and that promote compliance rather than avoidance or fraud. To meet people's rising expectations, policy making must also be a process of continuous learning and improvement.

Identifying the problem

3. Like some other countries the United Kingdom has, over the past 20 years, implemented a series of reforms in the work of government. The main focus has been on improving value for money in service delivery. Most of the nationalised industries have been privatised. Within central government, 'agencies' have been created: tasks have been more clearly defined, individuals offered more responsibility and managers given more scope to manage. Some of these tasks have also been privatised or contracted out. Local authorities have been subject to tight financial control and compulsory competitive tendering.

4. This emphasis on management reforms has brought improved productivity, better value for money and in many cases better quality services – all of which we are determined to build on. On the other hand, little attention was paid to the policy process and the way it affects government's ability to meet the needs of the people. Although there are areas, such as foreign and security policy, where effective co-ordination and collaboration are the norm, in general too little effort has gone into making sure that policies are devised and delivered in a consistent and effective way across institutional boundaries – for example between different government Departments, and between central and local government. Issues like crime and social exclusion cannot be tackled on a departmental basis. An increasing separation between policy and delivery has acted as a barrier to involving in policy making those people who are responsible for delivering results in the front line.

5.   Ministers are individually and collectively accountable to Parliament for the work of government. Too often, the work of Departments, their agencies and other bodies has been fragmented and the focus of scrutiny has been on their individual achievements rather than on their contribution to the Government's overall strategic purpose. Policies too often take the form of incremental change to existing systems, rather than new ideas that take the long-term view and cut across organisational boundaries to get to the root of a problem. The cultures of Parliament, Ministers and the civil service create a situation in which the rewards for success are limited and penalties for failure can be severe. The system is too often risk-averse.

What must change

6.   This Government expects more of policy makers. More new ideas, more willingness to question inherited ways of doing things, better use of evidence and research in policy making and better focus on policies that will deliver long-term goals. Our challenge, building on existing good practice, is to get different parts of government to work together, where that is necessary, to deliver the Government's overall strategic objectives – without losing sight of the need to achieve value for money. This means developing a new and more creative approach to policy making, based on the following key principles:

- **Designing policy around shared goals and carefully defined results, not around organisational structures or existing functions.** Many policies are rightly developed and pursued by a single part of government. But a focus on outcomes will encourage Departments to work together where that is necessary to secure a desired result.

- **Making sure policies are inclusive.** We will devise policies that are fair and take full account of the needs and experience of all those – individuals or groups, families and businesses – likely to be affected by them.

- **Avoiding imposing unnecessary burdens.** Where government considers it right to regulate it will do so, but regulation for its own sake is too often seen as an easy answer, without proper consideration being given to better ways of achieving the outcome. We will base our decisions on a careful appraisal of the benefits any measure seeks to achieve, the costs it entails and the cumulative burden of regulation on business. In doing so, we will give business and other interested parties a proper opportunity to contribute.

- **Involving others in policy making.** Rather than defending policies, government should lead a debate on improving them. This means developing new relationships between Whitehall, the devolved administrations, local government and the voluntary and private sectors; consulting outside experts, those who implement policy and those affected by it early in the policy making process so we can develop policies that are deliverable from the start.

- **Improving the way risk is managed.** Government is often criticised for intervening too much to protect people from some risks, while failing to protect them sufficiently from others. Much government activity is concerned with managing risks, in the workplace, in what we eat and in protecting the environment. We need consistently to follow good practice in policy making as we assess, manage and communicate risks.

- **Becoming more forward- and outward-looking.** This means learning to look beyond what government is doing now; improving and extending our contingency planning, learning lessons from other countries; and integrating the European Union and international dimension into our policy making.

- **learning from experience.** Government should regard policy making as a continuous, learning process, not as a series of one-off initiatives. We will improve our use of evidence and research so that we understand better the problems we are trying to address. We must make more use of pilot schemes to encourage innovations and test whether they work. We will ensure that all policies and programmes are clearly specified and evaluated, and the lessons of success and failure are communicated and acted upon. Feedback from those who implement and deliver policies and services is essential too. We need to apply the disciplines of project management to the policy process.

Taken together and if applied consistently, these principles will re-invigorate our policy making capacity and capabilities. But that is not the end of the story. This White Paper will form the start of an ongoing debate, involving Ministers, civil servants and other stakeholders, about how policy making can be improved and how we can best ensure that policy delivers the changes that really matter.

Making a start

7.   The **Comprehensive Spending Review** published last year, set new priorities for public spending with significant extra investment in key services such as education and health. It also identified key, cross-cutting issues that are best tackled across organisational boundaries. It is important that we build on this foundation to set clear priorities and a strategy for government as a whole.

Cross-cutting policy in practice – Sure Start

The Comprehensive Spending Review showed that services for children under 4 years old are patchy and fragmented. Research demonstrates that early intervention and support is important in reducing family breakdown; in strengthening children's readiness for school; and in preventing social exclusion and crime. The aim is to work with parents and children to improve the physical, intellectual, social and emotional development of young children.

Cross-departmental groups, involving people with an interest in health, education, the local environment, juvenile crime and family welfare as well as local government and the voluntary sector, were set up to devise and implement Sure Start. They have come up with an initial programme of 60 pilot projects – announced in January – based on evidence of what works and on the principle of learning from those with a track record in delivery.

---

8.   To help us learn what works best in policy making, we are also experimenting with different ways of organising work around cross-cutting issues.

> *Different ways of tackling cross-cutting policies*
>
> - *The **Social Exclusion Unit** is a cross-departmental team based in the Cabinet Office set up to tackle in a joined up way the wide range of issues which arise from the inequalities in society today.*
>
> - *The **Women's Unit** supports the Minister for Women in representing the needs of women within government through research, specific project work, timely interjections into policy initiatives and longer-term work on institutional change.*
>
> - *The **Performance and Innovation Unit** reports direct to the Prime Minister on selected issues that cross departmental boundaries, and proposes policy innovations to improve the delivery of the Government's objectives. It will also review aspects of government policy, with an emphasis on improving the co-ordination and practical delivery of policy and services which involve more than one public body.*
>
> - *The **crime reduction programme** relies on co-ordinated working across central and local government, drawing on their expertise in policy development, implementation and research, to identify and deliver effective measures for reducing crime.*
>
> - *The **UK Anti-drugs Co-ordinator** was appointed in 1997 to re-invigorate our approach to drugs problems and to galvanise the work of all agencies, ensure greater effectiveness and better use of resources.*
>
> - ***Customs & Excise/Inland Revenue** have agreed cross-representation on each other's Boards and appointed a joint programme director to improve co-ordination of their tax policies, secure increased compliance and deliver better and more efficient services to businesses.*
>
> - *The **Small Business Service** will improve the quality and coherence of delivery of government support programmes for small business and ensure they address their needs.*
>
> - *The Home Office, the Lord Chancellor's Department and the Crown Prosecution Service are now jointly planning and managing the **criminal justice system** (CJS) as a whole, including the publication for the first time of integrated plans for the CJS.*

9.   We need an effective system of **incentives and levers** to put these principles into practice and to tackle the barriers to more effective policy making. These may include new accountability arrangements, such as pooled budgets across Departments, cross-cutting performance measures and appraisal systems which reward team-working across traditional boundaries. We have asked the **Performance and Innovation Unit** (PIU) to examine the accountability and incentives framework and report its findings by the summer.

10.   The Government has taken a number of other steps already to apply these principles to policy making. For example:

- To make sure our policies are forward-looking, we have launched a new round of the cross-Departmental **UK Foresight Programme**. The PIU is separately identifying the key future challenges that government will have to face. This work will help Departments and other organisations to look beyond their existing policies towards the Government's long-term goals.

Looking ahead – the UK Foresight Programme

This will develop visions of the future, drawing in views from different age groups, regions and the widest possible range of organisations – government, the scientific community, business and the voluntary sector – to consider longer-term social, economic and environmental issues facing the UK. The aim is to help stakeholders, including government Departments, to identify what we need to do now, in partnership, to prepare us for future challenges and to make the most of advances in science and technology.

The Foresight 'knowledge pool', the first system of its kind in the world, will operate both as an electronic library of strategic visions, information and views about the future and as a platform for stimulating action by bringing people together and forging new partnerships.

- In the past, important groups in society have been marginalised. By understanding the diverse needs of society and mainstreaming them into Departments' thinking, we will be able to make policy that is better for all. As a first step, the Department for Education and Employment, the Home Office and the Women's Unit have issued new guidelines which set out how to achieve fair and inclusive policies, taking account of the needs of different groups in society. The new devolved administrations in Scotland, Wales and Northern Ireland will all have explicit remits to promote equality of opportunity in exercising their responsibilities.

- We will continue to draw the public, outside experts and those who implement policies into the policy making process through a range of task forces and review groups and by appointing lay members to many expert advisory committees.

Involving the public – Excellence in Schools

In order to ensure that all parents had the opportunity to contribute to the consultation Excellence in Schools (the Government's proposals for raising standards in schools in England by 2002) the Department for Education and Employment realised that they had to do more than publish an official paper. The proposals were produced in a number of formats and disseminated through many different outlets. A special telephone helpline was opened, free summaries were distributed through supermarkets and high street shops and there was a four-page pull-out section in the Sun newspaper. The helpline took over 1,700 calls, there were over 3,000 written responses to the full White Paper and a further 5,000 to the summary version. Most encouraging was the positive response, 3,500 replies, from individual parents. All responses were analysed and taken into account when decisions were reached.

St Mary's College Londonderry.

Southwark Council – Library and Information Services.

11. It is important to link the better ways of developing policy identified in this chapter to better ways of delivering policy through well-considered legislation. Our efforts have focused primarily on publishing more legislation in draft for consultation, and arranging formal pre-legislative scrutiny of draft Bills within Parliament where appropriate. A full set of explanatory notes is provided with each government Bill and we have introduced a statutory requirement for all Bills to be accompanied by a statement on compatibility with the European Convention on Human Rights. We have also taken a positive approach to modernising Parliamentary procedure in Westminster and are seeking to make use of some innovative procedures – such as the special Standing Committee on the Immigration and Asylum Bill – this Session.

Future action

12. The Government will go further to ensure that policy making delivers creative, robust and flexible policies, focused on outcomes. Action to achieve this will include:

- following up the start made in the Comprehensive Spending Review by looking in the next review of public spending plans for **further areas where joint working and budgeting** are appropriate.

- responding to the report by the Performance and Innovation Unit in the summer on **accountability and incentives** to tackle the barriers to joined up policy making and innovative team-working in service delivery and publishing the further action the Government intends to take in the light of that report.

- seeking further opportunities to improve all stages of the **legislative process**, from policy development, through Parliamentary consideration of legislation, to ways of keeping legislation up to date in a world of increasingly rapid change.

- producing and delivering an **integrated system of impact assessment and appraisal tools** in support of sustainable development, covering impacts on business, the environment, health and the needs of particular groups in society.

- developing, in the newly formed Civil Service Management Committee of Permanent Secretaries, a more **corporate approach** to achieving cross-cutting goals and providing the **leadership** needed to drive cultural change in the civil service. One of its tasks will be to ensure that the principles of better policy making are translated into staff selection, appraisal, promotion, posting and pay systems. (We discuss this further in chapter 6).

- offering, for the first time through the new Centre for Management and Policy Studies (see chapter 6), **joint training to Ministers and officials** which will allow them to discuss the way policy is, and should be, made and to address particular areas of policy. It will also promulgate **good practice** in policy making, and develop a more government-wide, outcome-focused culture.

- asking the Centre for Policy and Management Studies to organise a programme of **peer reviews** to ensure Departments implement the principles of Modernising Government. We will also consider how best to assess whether Departments are operating the management systems necessary to deliver the principles identified in this chapter.

- learning the lessons of successes and failures by carrying out more **evaluation of policies and programmes.** We will modernise evaluation standards and tools.

13. The Government is also introducing a series of steps aimed at removing unnecessary regulation and ensuring that future regulations are limited to measures which are necessary and proportionate. In particular:

- the Better Regulation Task Force will complement its existing role by spearheading a **new drive to remove unnecessary regulation**.

- we will introduce **legislation** to increase the flexibility of the Deregulation and Contracting Out Act 1994, to facilitate deregulatory action.

- where departments are preparing policies which impose regulatory burdens, **high quality Regulatory Impact Assessments** must be submitted to Ministers and the Cabinet Office must be consulted (in the same way as the Treasury is on proposals with public expenditure implications) before decisions are taken. This process should ensure that any new regulations do not impose unnecessary burdens and can be managed so as to minimise cumulative effects and business uncertainty.

3. Responsive public services

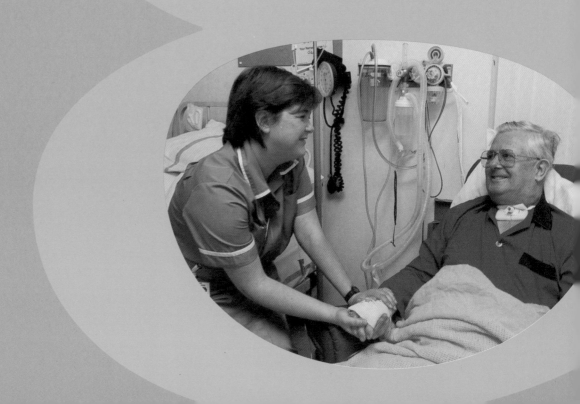

3. Responsive public services:

We will deliver public services to meet the needs of citizens, not the convenience of service providers

1.   Modernising Government means making sure that citizens and businesses come first. It means a genuine partnership between those providing services and those using them. People have grown impatient of barriers to effective and convenient service that stem simply from the way government is organised. They should not have to worry about what part of government they are dealing with. We must deliver services and programmes that are not only efficient and effective but also joined up and responsive. People have grown used to services being available when they want them. The Government is committed to making public services available 24 hours a day, seven days a week, where there is a demand. In short, we want public services that respond to users' needs and are not arranged for the provider's convenience.

Identifying the problem

2.   Research with the People's Panel (see paragraph 7) shows that more people agree than disagree that our public service providers are friendly, hard-working and keen to help. But, although the number of people who are satisfied is increasing, many services still fall short of expectations. Two out of five people think services have got no better in the last five years, and over one in three thinks they have become worse.

3.   There are many barriers to providing services in the way people want them. The separation of government into different units – though necessary for administrative purposes – often means that people do not receive services in a co-ordinated way or that they receive multiple visits from different agencies. Individual agencies' performance targets and budgets can get in the way of them working together. Audit and inspection processes may hinder cross-cutting work (see chapter 4). Different government offices are often situated a long way apart from one another, and attempts to bring them together can be hampered by rules and regulations. And the multiplicity of administrative boundaries across the country can lead to inefficiency, complication and confusion.

4.   Earlier this year, a number of '**Integrated-Service Teams**' were set up to identify the practical problems facing people when they use public services. The teams looked at seven of the most common 'life episodes': leaving school; having a baby; becoming unemployed; changing address; retiring; needing long-term care at home; and bereavement. Some of the most common problems were:

- People had to give the **same information more than once** to different – or even the same – organisations. A mother of a boy with physical disabilities said: "I have lost count of the times I have had to recount my son's case history to professionals involved in his care."

- There is often **no obvious person to help** those most in need to find their way around the system.

- There is a **lack of integrated information** to enable service providers to give a full picture of what help might be available.

- There is **minimal use of new technology**. Most government Departments have a website, but few allow people to fill in forms on line. And government websites are not well linked to other relevant sites.

5. The number of organisations a person needing long-term care may have to deal with is well illustrated by the diagram below.

NEEDING LONG-TERM DOMICILIARY CARE

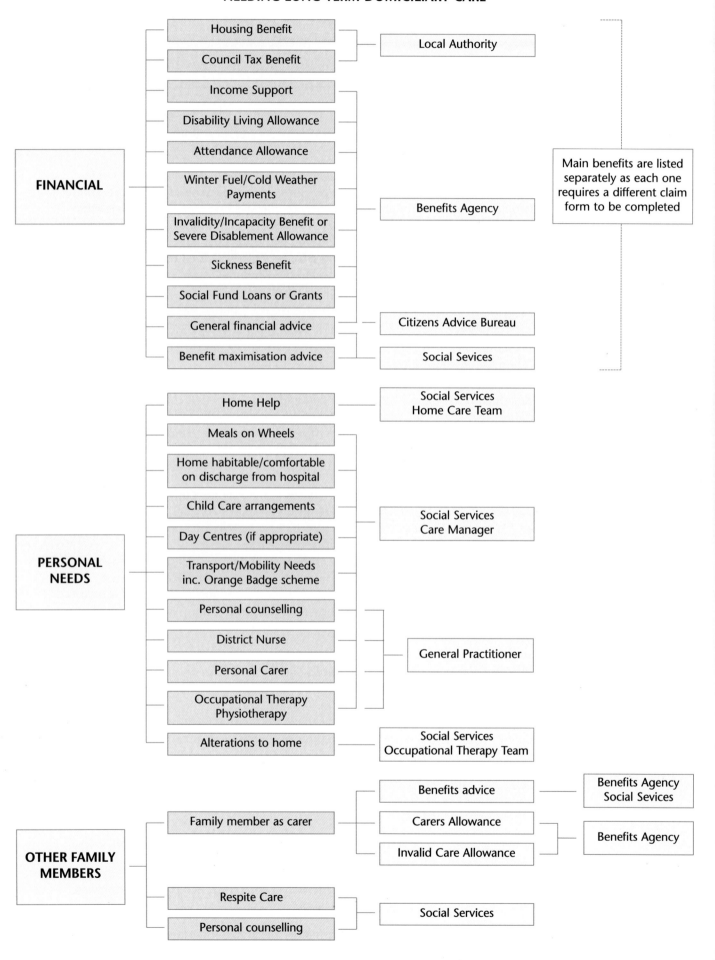

NOTE: This diagram is for illustration only. The list is not exhaustive and other organisations, friends and family may provide alternative services to those shown.

What must change

6. The Government wants public services that:

- **listen to people's concerns** and involve them in decisions about how services should be provided.

- **are sensitive to the needs of particular groups of people or businesses.**

- **reflect people's real lives.** Government should be organised so that people don't have to **hunt** down services by a process of trial and error.

- **make it easy to complain and get a result when things go wrong.**

Making a start

Listening to people

7. If public services are to serve people better, the Government needs to know more about what people want. Rather than imposing solutions we must consult and work with people. That is why we have set up the **People's Panel**: a 5,000-strong nationally representative group – a world first – to tell us what people really think about their public services and our attempts to make them better. The Panel supplements research being carried out by individual parts of government, including local initiatives such as citizens' juries, community fora and focus groups. We will also build in the views of customers when measuring the progress that Departments are making against their performance targets in their Public Service Agreements.

Central government

8. **Government Departments and agencies** must be sensitive to their customers. This is true even of organisations whose work does not bring them into daily contact with the public. The Government set six standards in 1997 to improve central government's response to the public. We have now reviewed these and have added new commitments. We will also set new targets to improve correspondence handling across central government.

Hereford and Worcester – Employment Service.

Bridgend and Glamorgan – Employment Service.

New service standards for central government

In serving you, every central government Department and agency will aim to:

- *answer your letters quickly and clearly. Each Department and agency will set a target for answering correspondence (including letters, faxes, and e-mails) and will publish its performance against this target.*

- *see you within 10 minutes of any appointment you have made at its office; it will *set a target for seeing callers without appointments, and publish performance against this target.*

- *answer telephone calls quickly and helpfully. *Each Department and agency will set a target for answering calls to telephone enquiry points, and will publish its performance against this target.*

- *provide clear and straightforward information about its service and those of related providers, along with one or more telephone enquiry numbers and *e-mail addresses to help you or to put you in touch with someone who can.*

- *have a complaints procedure – or procedures – for the services it provides, publicise it, including on the Internet, and send you information about it if you ask.*

- *do everything reasonably possible to make its services available to everyone, including people with special needs. Consult users and potential users regularly about the service it provides and report on the results.*

*These commitments will take effect on 1 October 1999.

Catering for the needs of different groups

9. Many people who use public services have particular needs or problems: for example, families, older people, women, ethnic communities and people with disabilities. The Government is determined that public services should address the needs of all groups.

10. Many older people find public services remote and intimidating. To give them a greater voice, the Government has set up the **Better Government for Older People** programme. We have also set up a Ministerial Group on Older People to ensure that Departments work together to respond to their needs. As part of the UN Year of Older Persons, Ministers will take part in a series of listening events for older people. And the new Performance and Innovation Unit has an Active Ageing Project, which will report in the autumn on how to improve the well-being and quality of life of older people by helping them remain active.

Newlon Housing Trust.

Walsgrave Hospitals NHS Trust – Occupational Therapy Department.

11. The Government has recognised the distinct interests and concerns of women by appointing a Minister for Women at Cabinet level. And initiatives such as the National Childcare Strategy and the National Minimum Wage have been designed with women at the forefront of our thinking. Future policies and services need to reflect the realities of women's daily lives, and should change as priorities and attitudes change. To help achieve this, the Minister for Women launched a **Listening to Women exercise** on 22 February 1999. This consists of regional road shows, a national conference of women's organisations, qualitative research, and a postcard campaign. Government has never communicated with women in this way before. We will circulate our findings in the autumn to all parts of government so that they can use them in their own policy making, and will develop women-specific guidelines for service providers.

12. The Government also recognises the needs of ethnic minorities. The Stephen Lawrence Inquiry, published in February 1999, starkly illustrated the need to rebuild the confidence of ethnic minority communities in public services. The Home Secretary has published his action plan setting out the programme of work in response to the inquiry's findings. When Parliamentary time permits, the Government will put beyond doubt that public services and law enforcement will be covered by race discrimination legislation.

13. Ethnic minority communities have already been given a voice at the heart of government through the establishment last June of the Home Secretary's Race Relations Forum. Its 28 members, drawn from a wide spectrum of experience, have already considered how to deliver better services, including how to improve the educational achievement of young people from ethnic communities. The Forum has close links with the Department for Education and Employment's Advisory Group on Raising Ethnic Minority Pupil Achievement.

14. For families, the consultation document, *Supporting Families*, published in November 1998, sought views on how to make services more family-friendly.

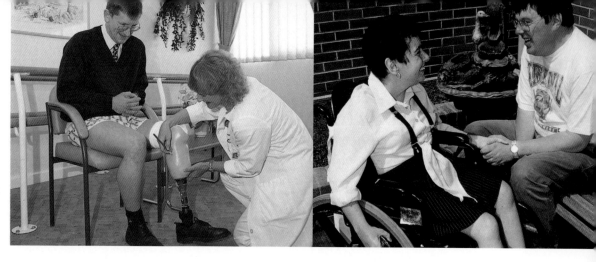

Preston acute hospitals NHS Trust – Disablement Services Centre

Care being provided at the Bexley Council Whitehall Centre

Services that reflect business needs

15. Many of the problems identified through the Integrated-Service Teams apply equally to businesses – especially small businesses – when they have to deal with government. The Government will establish a new Small Business Service, designed to provide the kind of practical help that smaller businesses need. The Department of Trade and Industry will consult small businesses, their representative organisations and other interested parties to make sure that the new body provides high quality services and support to small firms. The new service will have over £100 million of new money over the next three years for this purpose. Its role will be to:

- act as a strong voice for small business at the heart of government.

- improve the quality and coherence of delivery of government support programmes for small businesses and ensure that they address their needs.

- help small firms deal with regulation, working with others such as the Inland Revenue and Customs & Excise to cut the burdens of compliance.

Services that reflect real lives

16. Over the past two years, the Government has launched a range of new programmes to improve the joined up delivery of services both to individuals and to businesses. We have created Service First – the new Charter programme. We are tackling the problems of particularly deprived areas. And we are combining government's resources – at all levels – with those of the voluntary and private sectors.

17. We are setting up:

- **national, citizen-focused** programmes. Managed centrally by government Departments or agencies, these will cover the whole country, and will be available to all. Examples include NHS Direct and Employment Service Direct.

- **group-focused programmes**. These may be national or area-based, but are concerned with the needs of particular groups of people, such as the Better Government for Older People pilots, the New Deal for the Young Unemployed, or the Service Families Task Force.

- **area-based programmes.** These tackle the problems of particular areas or localities. Some have relatively large area boundaries (such as Health Action Zones and the Local Government Association's New Commitment to Regeneration). Others may be more locally based (such as Employment Zones, Education Action Zones, the New Deal for Communities and, in Wales, People in Communities). They are often targeted on areas of multiple deprivation.

Education Action Zones

In England, Education Action Zones (EAZs) will support schools by bringing them together with local businesses, local councils and others in an Action Forum. Each zone will typically cover between 15 and 25 schools (usually two or three secondary schools and their feeder primaries) and will be set up for three to five years. EAZ schools are able to innovate to raise standards, for example by introducing new approaches to rewarding teachers, including Advanced Skills Teachers, or an altered curriculum. The Action Forum could even act as a governing body for some of the schools. Twenty-five EAZs have already been established, and applications for more were invited in January 1999.

18. The aims and timetables for these initiatives differ. But they all share some common principles. They depend on partnership between different agencies in the public, private and voluntary sectors, and often involve users and staff too. They encourage experimentation and innovation. They make access to services easier for citizens and for businesses. By working together with other services, each organisation can make more effective use of its resources. And they encourage the spread of good practice. Above all, they are designed to make a difference on the ground. They have measurable outcomes, such as improving healthcare and giving better value for money. The Government will make sure they do.

One-stop shops

19. One-stop shops make life easier for those who use services. They can take the form of places people visit to get advice and information about different services, such as the Public Record Office's Family Records Centre and the Lewisham and Camden one-stop shops for benefits. Or they can be 'virtual' one-stop shops, available via the telephone or the Internet, such as the MOD's Veterans' Advice Unit, or Business Links. They reduce the number of separate visits people have to make to get services. They also lead to a more efficient use of resources by service providers.

Lewisham one-stop shop

People in Lewisham can now claim Income Support and Housing Benefit together on an electronic claim form, either in the Benefits Agency or local authority office, or by tele-claim to Belfast. This gives choice, uses new technology, and removes the need to deal with two separate organisations. Information is passed between the two electronically, rather than by paper. This speeds up decisions on financial help and delivers joined up service. People now receive one visit only, during which information for both parties is gathered. To get advice and help, people can choose to use video conferencing booths or call either the Benefits Agency or local authority office. This joined up approach is starting to provide a one-stop service for people in the area.

Camden one-stop shop

Lone parents living in Camden can now claim for Income Support, Child Support and Housing and Council Tax Benefit together, using a tele-claim to a call centre. This means they no longer have to provide much the same information separately to three organisations. Following the tele-claim, the lone parent receives one filled-in form for checking and signing. They can also get help about the New Deal for Lone Parents. This provides a better service, which is welcomed by lone parents, improves accuracy and speed of help, and involves staff positively.

Veterans' Advice Unit

The Ministry of Defence has launched a Veterans' Advice Unit to provide a telephone focal point for the United Kingdom's estimated 15 million ex-Service men and women and their dependants. The Unit acts as a one-stop shop or 'signpost' to advise callers on how to obtain expert help on issues of concern to them, whether provided by central or local government or voluntary organisations. It has handled calls on a wide range of issues including housing, finance, tracing of relatives and pensions.

Pooled budgets

20. The Government has set up a number of cross-departmental budgets involving several Departments in delivering programmes such as Sure Start and the New Deal for Communities. And we are taking steps, through the Health Bill and the Local Government Bill, to build on existing work, such as the Single Regeneration Budget, to help local agencies work together to support innovative service delivery by establishing pooled budgets.

Invest to Save Budget

21. The Government will spend £230 million over the next three years to fund projects that involve two or more public bodies getting together to deliver services that are more innovative, more joined up, more locally responsive and more efficient. About half the projects funded so far are piloting new ways of joint working that have the potential to be used more widely within the public sector.

Future action

22. The Government will take its drive for more joined up and responsive services further by:

- actively encouraging **initiatives to establish partnership delivery** by all parts of government in ways that fit local circumstances; and establishing common targets, financial frameworks, IT links and so on that support such arrangements.

- launching a second round of bids to the **Invest to Save Budget**, which will be available to the wider public sector (local authorities, health bodies, Non- Departmental Public Bodies and police authorities) as well as to central government.

- ensuring that all public bodies are **properly and fully accountable to the public**. The Parliamentary Ombudsman's jurisdiction has been extended to cover an additional 158 public bodies. To ease public access and improve efficiency in dealing with complaints across different services, we will also review the organisation of public sector ombudsmen in England.

- implementing a **community planning process** so that local authorities and other local public bodies can adopt a common and co-ordinated approach to meeting local needs.

- consulting on radical **improvements in the provision of registration services**, particularly with respect to user-friendliness, use of IT, and links to other services.

23. The Government will also tackle the barriers to joint working, by:

- producing an action plan by the summer on the lessons learned from the **Integrated-Service Teams'** experiences of practical problems faced by people using public services, including a commitment for people to be able to notify different parts of government of details such as a change of address simply and electronically in one transaction.

- launching, in April, a **network of local partnerships** to identify where central requirements for information get in the way of joint working, and exploring how performance measures can be used to support partnerships. The project will run until October 2000, and will share lessons widely across government.

- responding to the **Performance and Innovation Unit's** study in the summer on the way central government is organised and delivers services at regional and local level.

- developing a more co-ordinated approach to **property management**, so that people do not have to visit offices some distance from one another to get related services. We want property to be managed more flexibly, so that service providers can be more innovative in achieving joined up services. The Property Advisers to the Civil Estate (PACE) will take on a much stronger role in ensuring a joined-up approach. It will do this, across government, by developing an interactive common database for the government's estate that will allow Departments to share information and best practice via the Government Secure Intranet or the Internet; and by working with the Local Government Association to achieve a more co-ordinated approach across the public sector.

- working to align **the boundaries of public bodies**. More than 100 different sets of regional boundaries are used in England alone. This complicates administration, reduces efficiency and frustrates joined up government. It also confuses the public. Wherever possible, boundaries should coincide with local authority boundaries at local level, and with Government Office regions' boundaries at regional level. The Government will work from a presumption that geographical boundaries should be aligned in this way whenever public bodies next review their administrative, managerial or delivery arrangements and structures. We will only make exceptions when there are strong over-riding considerations, for example where we have already committed ourselves as a result of recent reviews. We expect all newly created bodies to aim to meet these requirements from the outset and will review progress in 2002.

24. The Government is determined to ensure that public services reflect real lives. We intend to bring about a significant transformation over the coming years:

Health – by the end of 2000, everyone in the country will be able to phone NHS Direct, 24 hours a day, for healthcare advice and information from experienced, qualified nurses.

Jobs – by 2001, jobseekers should be able to look for and apply for jobs through the Employment Service anywhere in England, Scotland and Wales using the telephone or Internet, including evenings and weekends.

Learning – by 2002, students of all ages will be able to access the National Grid for Learning, through all schools, colleges, universities, public libraries and as many community centres as possible so as to share high quality learning materials and have access to the wider Internet.

Older people – by the end of 2000, older people should benefit from joined up services and integrated planning in at least half our local authorities.

Changing address – a committment for people to be able to notify different parts of government of details such as a change of address simply and electronically in one transaction.

New benefit claimants – new benefit claimants will be able to deal with their employment needs and benefit claims in one place through the Single Work-Focused Gateway, eliminating the current duplication and confusion.

4. Quality public services

4. Quality public services:

We will deliver efficient, high quality public services and will not tolerate mediocrity

1.   This Government believes in the public service and public servants. But that does not mean the public service at any price. The British public has grown accustomed to consumer choice and competition in the private sector. If our public service is to survive and thrive, it must match the best in its ability to innovate, to share good ideas and to control costs. Above all, the public service must deliver efficiently and effectively the policies, programmes and services of government. Some of our public services achieve this now. But others do not. We intend to bring them up to the level of the best, and make the best even better, by modernising the controls under which they operate, by encouraging new ways of working and wherever practicable by giving the public the right to choose.

Identifying the problem

2.   Governments have not always looked closely enough at the link between spending and what the public is really getting in the way of results. Sometimes they have cut resources in one area without being fully aware of what the consequences across the system will be. At other times, resources have been increased with no real certainty that this is leading to improvements in services as experienced by users. The checks and controls that should drive improvement have been allowed to act instead as barriers to innovation. The incentives to modernise have been weak. And without having a clear enough picture of the outcomes on the ground, it has been difficult to identify lessons and share learning about how to do things better.

What must change

3.   The Government needs to ensure that public bodies are clearly focused on the results that matter to people, that they monitor and report their progress in achieving these results and that they do not allow bureaucratic boundaries to get in the way of sensible co-operation. We must make clear that additional investment comes with strings attached and is conditional on achieving improved results through modernisation. We must encourage a commitment to quality and continuous improvement, and ensure that public bodies know how to turn this commitment into results. And we must work in partnership with the independent audit bodies and inspectorates, so that we all focus on the goal of improving the value delivered to the public.

4.   Too often in the past, the tendency in the public service has been to stick with the traditional. The world is changing too fast for that to be an effective approach. The best public bodies have shown an ability to innovate and improve. We need to encourage others to follow the example of the best, and to make a step change in the general standards of public services.

5.   We must not assume that everything government does has to be delivered by the public sector. The last Government adopted an approach to competition in the public sector which favoured privatisation for its own sake and damaged the morale and ethos of the public service. This Government will adopt a pragmatic approach, using competition to deliver improvements. This means looking hard – but not dogmatically – at what services government can best provide itself, what should be contracted to the private sector, and what should be done in partnership.

Making a start

6. The Government has developed a number of levers to drive up standards in public services:

- The **Comprehensive Spending Review** established a new approach to improving service delivery. We provided significant additional resources for key services and made it clear that this money would be used for modernisation and investment in reform.

- The new **Public Service Agreements** (PSAs) for the first time set out in detail what people can expect in return for this substantial new investment. In some areas, such as criminal justice and action against illegal drugs, results will only be delivered effectively if different organisations co-operate. Cross-cutting Public Service Agreements define what needs to be achieved through joint action.

Key manifesto pledges on service standards incorporated in PSA targets

- *to cut infant class sizes to 30 or under for 5, 6 and 7 years olds by September 2001.*

- *to reduce the time taken from arrest to sentence for persistent young offenders from 142 to 71 days.*

- *to cut NHS waiting lists by 100,000 over the lifetime of the Parliament and to deliver a consequential reduction in average waiting times by May 2002.*

- *to get 250,000 under 25 year olds off benefit and into work by using money from the windfall tax.*

- The Government has developed a new approach **to public expenditure planning and control**. In place of annual plans, we have – wherever possible – set firm three-year spending plans for Departments. To bring an end to the rush to spend money at the end of the financial year, we have increased the scope to carry forward unspent provision. The introduction of resource accounting and budgeting will replace the archaic use of cash-based accounting. This will mean better linkages between the resources we put in and what we achieve, and will increase the incentives for assets to be managed effectively.

- The Government is doing more to develop its commercial skills, so that we can work more productively in partnership with industry to get the best deal for users. In the defence field, our Smart Procurement Initiative will transform the way equipment is procured. Independent reviews of central government procurement and the Private Finance Initiative will together strengthen our performance by making better use of public-private partnerships and closer collaboration between organisations. In construction, we have put in place a three-year strategy for achieving excellence as a client, and are working jointly with the construction industry to re-think and improve our management of public sector projects. Altogether we are sharpening up co-ordination of government's commercial activities, making better use of our skills, and exercising more influence with suppliers.

- Ministers and their Departments will be held to delivery of the priorities set out in the PSAs. The Government will ensure that these priorities are cascaded through the **targets and measures** which will be set for all public bodies, in consultations with those who receive services. On both targets and inspections, we will focus on key outcomes and strike an appropriate balance between intervening where services are failing and giving successful organisations the freedom to manage.

The new mechanisms for managing delivery

- **Comprehensive Spending Review**, *setting out for the first time a co-ordinated set of objectives covering all public spending.*

- **Public Service Agreements**, *setting out for the first time firm targets for improving services over the next three years. Shifting the focus decisively from inputs to the outcomes that matter.*

- *New* **Cabinet Committee** *(PSX) monitoring progress on a regular basis with relevant Secretaries of State.*

- *New* **Public Service Productivity Panel** *bringing together public and private sector expertise to help Departments achieve the improvements necessary.*

- **Annual Report** *summarising progress for Parliament and the public.*

Four principles for performance management and inspection

- **Encourage a whole systems approach.** *We will put the focus on assessing improvements in the effectiveness and value for money of a whole system, such as the criminal justice system, not just in its constituent parts.*

- **Move from counting what goes in, to assessing what is being delivered.** *We will keep a tight rein on the management of resources. But we also need to know what is being achieved with the money spent. The targets for government Departments, as far as possible, are expressed either in terms of the end results or service standards, and we are working to develop measures for all levels of government which support this approach.*

- **Intervene in inverse proportion to success.** *The Government is not afraid to take action where standards slip. But we do not want to run local services from the centre. Where services deliver results we will give them greater freedom to innovate.*

- **Use the right information at the right level.** *We want managers to use performance measures to monitor and improve their organisations. We do not want them to feel swamped by information overload or bureaucratic requests for irrelevant data. We will use new technology to take a more streamlined approach to managing information in the public sector.*

7.   The Government is also determined to encourage innovation and share good practice. To do this:

- we are working closely with the **Public Audit Forum** – which represents all the national audit agencies – to find ways of encouraging more modern and effective forms of service delivery at local as well as central level. Auditors are rightly interested in whether organisations obtain value for money. We want them to be critical of opportunities missed by sticking with the old ways, and to support innovation and risk-taking when it is well thought through. We welcome the Forum's statement that the national audit agencies will respond positively and constructively to our Modernising Government initiative. **In future, people will no longer be able to use audit as an excuse for not delivering more co-ordinated and efficient services.**

- **we plan to get rid of unnecessary or outdated statutory burdens** on public services, which prevent them delivering a modern service. We propose to extend the Deregulation and Contracting Out Act 1994 to make it easier to remove burdens from public sector organisations. We will also streamline the collection and sharing of data so that we can better manage government information, for example to help target efforts in tackling social exclusion.

- **we will identify organisations which would benefit from being given additional scope to innovate, and consider how to give them appropriate freedoms.** We will do this in central government through the regular reviews of agencies and Non-Departmental Public Bodies (NDPBs). In local government, the second stage of the beacon councils initiative will involve giving additional freedom and flexibility to those councils which have shown an ability to excel. The Local Government Association's New Commitment to Regeneration Pathfinders are also considering what types of freedom and flexibility would support their aim of regenerating local communities. We will build on these approaches with other ways of allowing local service delivery units to explore new ways of working. We will encourage staff to come forward with suggestions for how services can be improved.

> **GEMS Scheme** – *The Ministry of Defence's staff suggestion scheme is the largest in the country. It offers cash awards of £25 to £10,000 or more to staff in the Ministry of Defence and the Armed Forces who have ideas that can improve the management and delivery of defence. The scheme generates ideas saving £15 million per annum and demonstrates that staff are full of good ideas.*

8. When things are being done well, we need to share good ideas across the great range of organisations delivering different public services. To that end:

- we have launched a **Public Sector Benchmarking Project** to spread use of the Business Excellence Model across the public sector. The Model is widely used by leading private sector companies, but for the public sector this project is the world leader in scale and ambition. It is helping to spread best practice across boundaries, not just within the public sector, but between public and private users of the Model and internationally. Take-up of the Model has already reached 65% of central government agencies and 30% of local authorities. Over 90% of users report that their rate of improvement has increased as a direct result.

- in the health sector, we are setting up the National Institute for Clinical Excellence to provide a single focus for guidance to clinicians about which treatments work best for which patients. Good practice in NHS Trusts and primary care will also be identified through the new NHS beacon services initiative.

- in local government, we have set out our plans to establish centres of excellence by introducing the beacon council scheme, designed to promote and recognise innovation in areas of cross-cutting work. In addition, the Local Government Improvement and Development Agency will act as champion of a best practice culture in local government.

- in education, beacon schools are piloting a range of initiatives to share ideas and approaches to teaching, and to pass on expertise in a host of subjects.

- we have developed principles of good regulation and enforcement. These recognise that regulations should be necessary, fair, effective, balanced and enjoy a broad degree of public support. The primary function of central and local government enforcement work is to protect the public, the environment and groups such as workers. But at the same time, we need to ensure that enforcement functions are carried out in an equitable, practical and consistent manner in order to promote a thriving national and local economy.

University Hospital Birmingham NHS Trust.

Birmingham City Council – Neighbourhood Advice & Information Service.

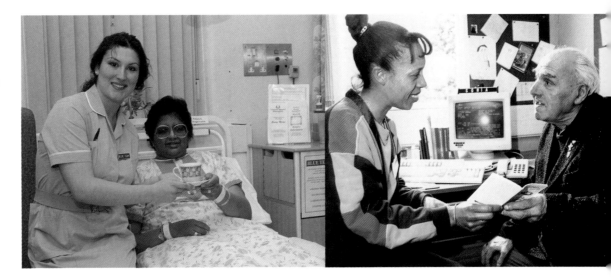

Future action

9.   The Government is committed to achieving **continuous improvement in central government policy making and service delivery**. To achieve this we have devised five principles: challenge, compare, consult, compete and collaborate. We will use these to build on our Best Value approach to local government and complement the existing scrutiny of central government carried out by the National Audit Office and by Parliament. We will offer these approaches as models for the devolved administrations to consider in developing their own approaches to continuous improvement.

Continuous improvement for central government	We will:
Challenge Is this service, legislation or policy work what is needed? Is it being delivered in the right way by the right organisation?	• assess the impact of policies and legislation (for example on ethnic minorities or small firms, or people's health) before they are introduced. We will also evaluate policies after they have been introduced and put right any failures. • (as set out in *Better Quality Services*) review all activities in all Departments and agencies against five options: abolish, restructure internally, strategically contract out, market test or privatise. • strengthen the five-yearly reviews of agencies and NDPBs.
Compare Compare actual performance with promises, and learn by benchmarking policy making and services between organisations, between regions, between sectors and between countries.	• use Public Service Agreements. These provide, for the first time, hard targets for improving services over the next three years. They shift the focus decisively from inputs to outcomes. • monitor progress on a regular basis through the new Cabinet Committee (PSX). • use the new Public Service Productivity Panel to bring public and private sector expertise together. • produce an Annual Report summarising progress. • benchmark service delivery and policy functions, in particular by using the Business Excellence Model.

Consult
 	
Be responsive to the needs of users, listen to and work with stakeholders, including both customers and staff.
	• consult stakeholders as part of our continuous improvement activity. This is:
	   – one of the nine principles of the Service First programme.
	   – the starting point for service level and organisational reviews.
	   – supported by publication of departmental and agency annual reports.
	   – part of best practice in developing and implementing policy and legislation.

Compete What matters is what works – the Government should use the best supplier whether public, private or voluntary sector.	• build on *Better Quality Services* which sets out the Government's pragmatic approach and provides guidance on how to achieve it. We will work with the Local Government Association to develop guidance on how Best Value and Better Quality Service reviews can be used together to help join up services. • base procurement on competition to secure best whole-life value. • use partnering to encourage innovation and continuous improvement, and PFI for capital projects.
Collaborate Work across organisational boundaries to deliver services that are shaped around user needs and policies that take an holistic approach to cross-cutting problems.	• build on the development of partnerships, at local level through initiatives such as Health Action Zones, and at national level, for example through a joint strategy for the criminal justice system. We are working to identify and overcome the barriers to closer working between organisations, as set out in chapter 2.

Best Value is currently being introduced to replace compulsory competitive tendering in local government. It is a rigorous system for delivering high quality, responsive services based on locally determined objectives and underpinned by performance measurement and independent inspection and audit in order to achieve continuous improvement.

10. **Improving the quality and efficiency of public services requires a new approach to the question of who should supply services.** In recent years, the application of compulsory competitive tendering and market testing has led too dogmatically to the use of private sector suppliers. Although it delivered savings and efficiencies, this was sometimes at the expense of quality. This Government will not make the mistake of rigidly preferring private sector delivery over public sector delivery, or vice versa. Instead, we will develop an approach based on the straightforward idea of best supplier, retaining an open mind about which supplier, public, private or partnership, can offer the best deal.

11. Over the next five years, we will review all central and local government department services and activities – by consulting widely with users, by benchmarking and by open competition – to identify the **best supplier** in each case. The focus will be on end results and service standards, rather than simply on processes. The aim will be to secure the best quality and value for money for the taxpayer. We also want clarity and certainty about the treatment of staff, and wherever there is a change of service provider we will support staff by presuming TUPE protections (Transfer of Undertakings Protection of Employment regulations) apply. Winning suppliers will need to offer improved quality, as well as better productivity and lower costs. And because public service needs do not stand still, we expect best suppliers to prove they can manage change and offer the public continuous improvement. We will mount a co-ordinated programme across the public sector based on common principles, embracing the Better Quality Services initiative for central departments and agencies, and Best Value in local government.

12. To make sure we get the best supplier, competition will be considered seriously as an option in every case. Where internal restructuring without competition emerges as the preferred solution, then for larger central government services, this will be subject to prior scrutiny by the Cabinet Office and Treasury. The Government will take decisive action to deal with failing services, whether supplied by the public or the private sector. A Committee of Ministers (PSX) will monitor the performance of Departments in delivery of Better Quality Services, ensuring that reviews are robust and generate continuous improvements in quality and cost.

Premier Health NHS Trust – Children's Centre.

Dyfed Powys – Community policing.

13. The Government will take other steps to **raise the quality of public services to the standards of the best**, and to make the best better. We will:

- encourage public sector organisations to adopt one of the main quality management schemes. They deliver real improvements, whether in customer service (Charter Mark), the skills and motivation of staff (Investors in People), services and processes (ISO 9000), or to the complete organisation (the Business Excellence Model).

Quality schemes

Barnsley Community and Priority Services NHS Trust *have 1998 Charter Mark, accreditation to ISO 9001 and IiP. These enable objective and independent evaluation of the Trust's services. Having the three awards enables the Trust to focus on different aspects of quality across the entire organisation.*

The London Borough of Southwark *uses four quality tools extensively. ISO 9000 is employed to improve processes and Charter Mark for units dealing with the public. The quality of service of Charter Marked units has noticeably improved. IiP is used to help staff achieve overall objectives; while the Business Excellence Model has been adopted to provide a strategic overview.*

The Land Registry's *mission is to be recognised as the most professional, efficient and courteous public service in the UK. It monitors progress through the Business Excellence Model, Charter Mark and IiP which collectively provide a comprehensive 'health check' – a rigorous set of standards which help planning and direct the drive for continuous improvement.*

- **ask the new Modernising Government Quality Schemes Task Force to report by the end of this year** on how the different quality schemes can work together in the public sector to enhance their overall impact.

- establish a new scheme to encourage Charter Mark holders and high-scoring users of the Business Excellence Model to stage open days for peer organisations building on the new beacon approach.

- change central government's approach to reviewing its agencies, and NDPBs (quangos). All such reviews will in future focus on outcomes, will take into account the views of customers, and look at the scope for improving services through collaboration. We will publish guidance on the new approach in the autumn.

Hereford & Worcester Fire Brigade.

Lancashire Ambulance Service NHS Trust

- collaborate with the Audit Commission and inspectorates to **develop principles of public inspection.** These principles should make clear that inspection has a positive role to play in supporting improvements in services as well as in providing assurance about standards.

- set up a new **Best Value Inspectorate Forum** in the summer as a means of **encouraging more co-operation between inspectorates.** We will encourage the Forum to look at whether inspectorates take sufficient account of joint working between the bodies they inspect; at the scope for involving users more in the inspection process; at the scope for co-ordinating their programmes and sharing information; and at how best to target their resources on those areas where the risks involved are greatest – intervention in inverse proportion to success. And we will encourage those inspectorates not involved in Best Value to act on lessons learned.

- launch a sponsored competition this year, based on the criteria of the Business Excellence Model, to encourage good practice in partnership working.

- bring together front-line staff from across the public sector in a regular forum with senior policy makers at the centre of government to ensure that policies can take better account of operational experience.

- set up a new website for sharing best practice which will include a database of good practice examples.

5. Information age government

5. Information age government:

We will use new technology to meet the needs of citizens and business, and not trail behind technological developments

1.   Information technology is changing our lives: the way we work, the way we do business, the way we communicate with each other, how we spend our time. New technology offers opportunities and choice. It can give us access to services 24 hours a day, seven days a week. It will make our lives easier. Government intends to be at the head of these developments, using them to give effect to the vision in this White Paper.

Identifying the problem

2.   We have seen a revolution over the past decade in the way leading companies across the world do business. They have used networked computing to refocus their activities on the customer. They have used IT to work more closely with their suppliers. They have made innovative use of information to become learning organisations. They have supplied new services, when, where and how the customer wants them. They have developed new delivery channels like call centres and the Internet. They have given their staff the support they need to use IT effectively.

3.   Government has not kept sufficient pace with these developments. We have been active in some areas. We set out our programme in a consultation paper, *Our Information Age*. We have launched major initiatives in education, libraries and the health service. We have begun to widen access to IT skills and to encourage the growth of electronic commerce and digital broadcasting. In the White Paper *Our Competitive Future* we have made clear our championship of electronic commerce as a key tool for a successful knowledge-driven economy. And in the Budget we announced a programme worth £1.7 billion to provide computers and IT literacy for all.

4.   But we must go much further. Government has so far followed a largely decentralised approach to IT development. This has allowed Departments and agencies to modernise their systems in ways that meet their own needs. But we have not developed ways of ensuring that we maximise the benefits of IT for government as a whole. As a result, we have incompatible systems and services which are not integrated. We must do more if we are to obtain the real benefits of information age government, for better service delivery, better procurement and more efficient working.

What must change

5.   The Government must bring about a fundamental change in the way we use IT. We must modernise the business of government itself – achieving joined up working between different parts of government and providing new, efficient and convenient ways for citizens and businesses to communicate with government and to receive services.

6.   Society is not homogeneous. Government exists to serve those who feel excluded from developments in information technology just as much as it serves those who embrace the new technology. The information age should increase the choice of how citizens and businesses receive services, not restrict it. The Internet, interactive TV and touchscreen delivery should take their place alongside more innovative use of the telephone, the call centre and the paper document, not replace them; nor should face to face contact be replaced where that is what is needed. **We will develop targeted strategies to ensure that all groups have proper access to information age government.**

Making a start

A corporate IT strategy for government

7.   We are developing a **corporate IT strategy for government**. IT systems have tended to be developed separately by different public service agencies; we need now to encourage them to converge and inter-connect. This will focus on the needs of citizens and businesses and will encourage wider choice on how public services should be provided. It will maximise the benefits to both central and local government of a more co-ordinated approach to information technology procurement. In taking it forward we will work in partnership across the public sector and with the private sector. Through the strategy the Government will:

- set key objectives for managing, authenticating and identifying data, using commercial open standards wherever possible.

- establish frameworks for specific technologies where stronger co-ordination is needed.

- ensure that government acts as a champion of electronic commerce.

E-commerce

By 2002, UK businesses and customers will be working in the best economy in the world for electronic trading. E-commerce is revolutionising the commercial world, offering greater choice to consumers, and greater access to markets for suppliers. In March 1999, the Government published a consultation paper proposing legislation for building confidence in e-commerce, and will be publishing a Bill after Easter.

- use the Government Secure Intranet (GSI) to boost cross-departmental working and to make the public sector work more coherently.

- strengthen the protection of privacy and human rights while providing a clear basis for sharing data between departments.

8. In taking forward this strategy, we will :

- designate a senior official at board level within each Department to champion the information age government agenda within the Department and its agencies.

- benchmark progress against targets for electronic service delivery, and against the best performance in the private sector and in other countries.

- continue to work closely with business, both bilaterally and through the Information Age Partnership and associated groups.

- incorporate information age government objectives into the approach for Best Value and beacon councils, and into agency framework documents.

- align expenditure which supports IT investment from the Invest to Save Budget and the Capital Modernisation Fund with the strategy.

- set a target that by the end of the year all Departments should be participating in the Government Secure Intranet. We will establish secure onward links to local authorities, hospitals and post offices. We will provide the IT base for government to work as a learning organisation and develop a range of applications on the GSI to support effective working across departmental boundaries. We will use the GSI as a platform for management of electronic government records.

Electronic services for citizens and businesses

9. The Government is taking specific actions to **develop information age government through IT** in a number of areas. In many cases this is allowing public services to be delivered 24 hours a day, seven days a week. We will continue to promote initiatives to modernise services in accordance with the needs of citizens and businesses.

For example:

- the NHS will use IT to transform the way health services are delivered. NHS Direct will achieve national coverage by the end of 2000.

- from 2000, individual taxpayers and businesses will be able to make income tax returns to the Inland Revenue and register for VAT with Customs & Excise over the Internet. In the Budget, the Government announced that there would be a discount for small businesses which make their tax returns electronically.

- citizens and businesses in Northern Ireland, will be able to use an integrated service for vehicle testing, licensing and insurance which is being established in partnership with the insurance industry.

Better health services through the NHS

From the end of April 1999, 20 million people will be able to call NHS Direct for healthcare advice from experienced, qualified nurses. NHS Direct will work in partnership with other local services to provide advice to callers about getting the right level of care.

Some healthcare professionals are now able to deliver quicker test results, up-to-date specialist advice and even online booking of appointments through NHSnet. They will, later this year, also get access to a wide range of health information through the National Electronic Library for Health.

Better service for taxpayers

Taxpayers whose affairs are handled by the Inland Revenue Centre at East Kilbride can expect a great improvement in the service they receive. In February 1999, the Inland Revenue opened its first dedicated call centre in East Kilbride, which will conduct a wide range of business for 2 million employees and pensioners. Access to a faster and more convenient service for the customer is accompanied by increased efficiency for the Inland Revenue. Alongside the call centre is an incoming-mail room which will also handle all the postal interactions with customers in the area, and a one-stop shop handling 33,000 visits a year. This separation of roles will allow the 'customer facing' office to focus solely on providing excellent service to the customer, while the 'back office' can focus on efficient processing of data.

National Grid for Learning

More and more people are able to access information on a wide range of educational resources through the National Grid for Learning. The Grid is the national focal point for learning on the Internet. It is both an architecture of educationally valuable content and a programme for developing the means to access it in schools, libraries, colleges, universities, workplaces, homes and elsewhere. The National Grid for Learning initiative aims to connect all schools to the Internet by 2002. Currently, 30% of primary schools, 90% of secondary schools and 45% of special schools in England have some form of Internet access. The Grid was launched in November 1998 by the Prime Minister. The National Grid for Learning site and its partners offer some 50,000–60,000 pages of material, and more is available each week. The site is currently being accessed on average over 75,000 times a day.

University for Industry

Individuals and businesses will soon have access to a wealth of lifelong learning resources through the University for Industry, a new kind of organisation for open and distance learning. Using modern information and communications technologies, it will broker high-quality learning products and services and make them available at home, in the workplace and at learning centres country-wide.

Llandough Hospital and Community NHS Trust.

Darlington College of Technolgy.

Partnership

10. We set out our plans to transform local government in the White Paper *Modern Local Government In Touch with the People*. We will expand on these by establishing a **Central/Local Information Age Government Concordat**, which will encourage innovation and co-operation between central and local service providers. It will drive up technology standards across the public sector.

11. We are also looking at how the public service can work in partnership with the private sector and voluntary organisations to deliver public services in innovative ways. We are talking to banks, the Post Office, supermarkets, accountants, interactive broadcasting companies, the information technology industry and others about how they can be partners in service delivery. Alongside this White Paper, the Central IT Unit of the Cabinet Office is publishing on the Internet a fuller description of this work.

Future action

Information age government for citizens and business

By 2002, the Government intends, as a minimum, that citizens will be able electronically to:

- *book driving and theory tests.*
- *look for work and be matched to jobs.*
- *submit self-assessment tax returns.*
- *get information and advice about benefits.*
- *get on-line health information and advice.*
- *use the National Grid for Learning.*
- *apply for training loans and student support.*

Business will be able electronically to:

- *complete VAT registration and make VAT returns.*
- *file returns at Companies House.*
- *apply for regional support grants.*
- *receive payments from government for the supply of goods and services.*

Framework policies across government

12. The Government will take forward its vision of information age government further by publishing a range of new frameworks across government to cover:

- **data standards**. We will put in place on the Government Secure Intranet standard definitions and programming tools to allow Departments to develop new systems in a consistent and standardised way, and to present the data they already hold in a common way.

- **digital signatures**. These can provide a means of identification and authentication when conducting business with government. We will legislate to ensure legal equivalence between digital and paper and pen signatures and work with financial institutions and others so that their digital signature products can be used to enable government transactions.

- **call centres**. A common approach to how people identify themselves when dealing with government call centres.

- **smartcards**. These can carry digital signatures and are increasingly capable of supporting many functions on the same card. We are working with banks and other partners to make them available for dealings with government. We will publish a framework for their use in support of service delivery across government.

- **digital TV**. How government should best develop services and information for delivery using digital TV.

- **web sites**. To bring about a more coherent approach to the use of web sites for giving information and eventually delivering services, we will publish guidelines for government websites by November 1999. We will relaunch the site www.open.gov.uk. so that it provides easier access to information and an updated search facility.

- **government gateways**. In the longer term, we aim to link the widest possible range of government services and information through electronic government **gateways** (or portals). Government agencies and Departments hold very large amounts of data. The variety of systems, some of them now old, makes accessing that data efficiently a key problem. Projects, such as the Department of Social Security's **ACCORD**, have begun to address these issues. We will build on this experience to manage information in support of better service delivery. A prototype government portal will be developed this year.

- **better on-line services for businesses**. The Government intends to make information about regulations more accessible from a single source and to increase greatly the scope for businesses to respond electronically to demands for information from government. This initiative will be taken forward by the new Small Business Service. We are funding a study into the development of a **single business register** from the Invest to Save Budget to provide electronic identification of businesses for their dealings with government.

Financial transactions between citizens and government

13. New technology provides an opportunity to simplify the increasingly complicated set of **financial transactions between citizens and government**. The closer integration of the tax and benefit systems, the development of a range of accounts to pay for training, and the creation of the Single Work-Focused Gateway, set new challenges. The Government will ensure as simple a set of transactions for the citizen as possible, avoiding duplication of effort by Departments and achieving best value for our investment. We will explore how we might promote social inclusion by encouraging greater use of the banking system. In support of these aims we propose:

- to promote access to and use of personal accounts, managed by banks and other institutions, by as broad a section of society as possible.

- to adopt as an aim across government that payments should usually be made into an account of the citizen's choice.

- to examine whether greater data sharing between Departments, agencies and local government will help them to provide easier financial dealings with citizens.

Privacy

14. There is concern that information technology could lead to mistaken identity, inadvertent disclosure and inappropriate transfer of data. The Government will address these concerns and will demonstrate our belief that **data protection is an objective of information age government, not an obstacle to it.**

On privacy, the Government will:

- *work closely with the Data Protection Registrar to ensure that privacy implications of electronic service delivery are fully addressed.*

- *carry through our commitment to openness, so that the citizen has relevant information about our initiatives as they are developed and implemented.*

- *promote specific codes of practice, on a departmental or inter-departmental basis, for information age government.*

- *benefit from the Data Protection Registrar's powers to conduct independent assessments of the processing of personal data.*

- *deploy privacy-enhancing technologies, so that data is disclosed, accessed or identified with an individual only to the extent necessary.*

- *provide a proper and lawful basis for data sharing where this is desirable, for example in the interest of improved service or fraud reduction consistent with our commitment to protect privacy.*

Electronic delivery

15. The Prime Minister announced in 1997 that, **by 2002, 25% of dealings with Government should be capable of being done by the public electronically.** Progress towards this target will be published on a six-monthly basis from May 1999 on www.citu.gov.uk. The target has been included in Departments' Public Service Agreements. Each Department's target will be reviewed on the basis of its returns for the May report. Where a target is insufficiently challenging it will be revised. We have also set a target that, by March 2001, 90% by value of low value purchases by central government should be carried out electronically.

16. The Government's aim is to ensure that the UK is at the forefront of international best practice. **We will set new targets** beyond 2002. Before we set the target for 2005, we will ask Departments to identify processes that for operational or policy reasons are incapable of delivery electronically, or for which there is genuinely unlikely to be demand. Those excepted, we propose **that 50% of dealings should be capable of electronic delivery by 2005 and 100% by 2008.** We believe that all local authorities should set and publish their own targets for electronic delivery and will begin discussions with the Local Government Association in order to bring this about. We are also monitoring the progress Departments are making to deliver information age government in an integrated way. Details of this work are on www.citu.gov.uk.

17. We know that we cannot picture now exactly what information age government will look like in 2008. The pace of technological change is fast and exhilarating. Business will be transformed by e-commerce. Before 2008, there will be further technological break-throughs which cannot be foreseen now. (In 1978, some commentators might not even have predicted the personal computer, let alone the Internet.) The Government's strategy must be flexible enough to take advantage of such developments, rather than locking citizens, business, government and our partners into rigid structures which may be overtaken.

18. But we can reasonably predict some of the elements which are likely to contribute to achieving the 100% target by 2008. **Here are ten drivers of information age government:**

- **Household access to electronic services** through developments such as interactive TV. But there will also be a very wide range of public access points, with advice on hand.

- Much more **user-friendly, inexpensive, and multi-functional technology** as TV, telephones and broadcasting converge.

- As part of this, **less dependence on keyboard skills** as remote control pads, voice command, touch screens, video-conferencing and other developments make it easier for users to operate and benefit from new technology. But other skills will be built up in schools, in the workplace, and across the community.

- Continuing **dramatic increases in computing power,** and in the power of networked computing, together enabling government services to be delivered more conveniently, accurately, quickly and securely.

- Wide scale take-up of **multi-purpose smartcards,** with which citizens can identify themselves, use services, safeguard their privacy and, increasingly, make and receive payments. Cards will also evolve into still more powerful technologies.

- Government **forms and other processes which are interactive,** guided by on-line help and advice, and collect all the necessary information in one go.

- **Smarter knowledge management** across government, which increasingly enables government to harness its data and experience more effectively, and to work in new ways.

- **Use of government web sites** and other access points as single gateways, often structured around life episodes, to a whole range of related government services or functions.

- **Repackaging of government services or functions**, often through partnerships with the private sector, local government or the voluntary sector, so that they can be provided more effectively.

- **Flexible invest to save approaches**, where the huge potential of new technology to increase efficiency is used imaginatively to fund better-designed processes.

19. Such developments will not limit choice, end face-to-face dealings or invade the privacy of the individual. Nor will they, in themselves, turn the complex issues which citizens and businesses face in the real world into simple ones, although they can radically improve services such as medical advice, education and training and crime reduction. Nevertheless, the potential for change is vast. **There is no good reason why, by 2008, it should not be as simple and easy to do many of the main dealings with government as it is today to make a phone call or choose between TV programmes.**

20. This vision must be turned into reality. We will build on the planned examples of electronic services in paragraph 9 by ensuring that an increasing number of services are capable of being delivered electronically in the next few years. In terms of implementation, the key elements are as follows:

- **A route map** and a set of **strategic enablers** will be provided by the corporate government IT strategy, together with the frameworks for data standards, digital signatures, call centres, smartcards, digital TV, web sites, government gateways and privacy, envisaged in this White Paper.

- Information age government services and other processes are likely to develop increasingly around **clusters of related government functions** aligned to the needs of citizens and businesses. As part of this, more services will become available 24 hours a day, seven days a week.

- This will be given impetus by **stronger central co-ordination**, to ensure that best practice and consistent standards are applied across government, that all the government bodies with an interest in a particular set of services come together to talk to potential partners, and that they promote compatibility across IT systems and data sets.

- **Progress against targets** will be regularly **monitored and reported**. At the same time, it is important that targets should not be viewed narrowly or purely incrementally. It will be necessary to plan further ahead to make the most of the opportunities for working across boundaries, partnership and service integration.

- Close **consultation and benchmarking** will continue with international, private sector and other colleagues. It is essential that the strategy should be implemented in ways which take full account of the changing environment and enable government to learn continuously from best practice elsewhere.

- **Market research** and **user feedback** will improve the design and organisation of services and other processes, and focus them more firmly on citizens and businesses.

6. Public service

6. Public service:

We will value public service, not denigrate it

1.   The Government is committed to public services and public servants. But, as we have said elsewhere in this White Paper, that does not mean an unchanging public service, a public service at any price. We have set out in chapter 4 how we will reward success, but not tolerate mediocrity. This means the public service must operate in a competitive and challenging environment. Public services and public servants must strive to be the best, and must make the best better still.

2.   The Government has a particular responsibility as employer. We will value the public service and make sure that it is properly equipped to rise to the challenge and properly rewarded when it does well. We will create a civil service for the 21st century. We must build the capability to change, and ensure that we have the leadership to bring it about.

3.   The Government has transformed the way it works with the public service trade unions. We recognise the contribution they can and do make to achieving shared goals. We will continue to work in partnership with them.

Identifying the problem

4.   Public service has for too long been neglected, undervalued and denigrated. It has suffered from a perception that the private sector was always best and the public sector was always inefficient. The Government rejects these prejudices. But their legacy remains.

5.   Despite that, public services have responded. The reforms of the last two decades in the civil service, for example, have done much to develop a more managerial culture. The quality of management has improved, there is a better focus on developing people to deliver improved performance and there is greater professionalism.

6.   But the world is changing rapidly and the demands placed on public servants are changing too. There is a wealth of goodwill and ability to build on. And we must not jeopardise the public service values of impartiality, objectivity and integrity. But we need greater creativity, radical thinking and collaborative working. We must all, both the politicians elected by the people and the officials appointed to serve, move away from the risk-averse culture inherent in government. We need to reward results and to encourage the necessary skills.

What must change

7.   The public service must be the agent of the changes identified throughout this White Paper. To do this it must have a culture of improvement, innovation and collaborative purpose. We will invest in public servants so that they have the skills and the opportunity to perform to the standards required. And we will remove unnecessary bureaucracy which prevents public servants from experimenting, innovating and delivering a better product.

8. If staff are to adopt new ways of working and a culture of continuous improvement, they must be rewarded for doing so. We must provide incentives for innovation, cross-cutting thinking, collaborative working and excellent service delivery. We must revise the core competencies for staff and appraisal systems to reflect the qualities we seek.

9. The Government must create an environment in which more of the brightest and best of each generation want to work in the public service. Public services must strike the right balance between identifying and bringing on internal talent and recruiting skills and experience from outside. Too much existing talent is wasted. Staff must not be denied the opportunity to demonstrate their potential and should be given sufficient responsibility at an early stage. We must identify the most talented early on, give them the opportunity to shine and promote the best much more quickly. We must also bring in new talent. Public services are, and will remain, for many people employers which provide a long-term career for those who want it and are able to meet the constantly changing demands. We want the civil service to reinforce its efforts to be more open and to recruit more experience, skills and ideas from outside. This must happen at all levels. We must be more flexible in bringing people in for short periods to provide specific skills for a particular policy area or project.

10. We must get more movement within the public service and with other sectors. There has been a long, and respectable, history of interchange between the civil service and other sectors. We must now change gear. We must do more to increase the number of secondments and involve people from other organisations in projects. We must review the current interchange targets and change them and provide new incentives and mechanisms to achieve them.

11. We must achieve greater diversity within the public service so that it can meet the varying needs within our diverse society.

Making a start

12. The Prime Minister set out seven challenges for the civil service at a conference in October 1998. In January 1999, at the Charter Mark Award ceremony, he began a dialogue with public servants more generally, on recruitment, retention and motivation.

Seven challenges for the civil service

- *Implementing constitutional reform in a way that preserves a unified civil service and ensures close working between the UK government and the devolved administrations.*

- *Getting staff in all Departments to integrate the EU dimension into policy thinking.*

- *Focusing work on public services so as to improve their quality, make them more innovative and responsive to users and ensure that they are delivered in an efficient and joined up way.*

- *Creating a more innovative and less risk-averse culture in the civil service.*

- *Improving collaborative working across organisational boundaries.*

- *Managing the civil service so as to equip it to meet these challenges.*

- *Thinking ahead strategically to future priorities.*

A learning organisation: training and development

13. The public service must become a learning organisation. It needs to learn from its past successes and failures. It needs consistently to benchmark itself against the best, wherever that is found. Staff must be helped to learn new skills throughout their careers.

> **Centre for Management and Policy Studies**
>
> *The new Centre for Management and Policy Studies, which will incorporate the Civil Service College, will:*
>
> - *be responsible for corporate civil service training and development.*
>
> - *ensure that the current and future leaders of the civil service are exposed to the latest ideas and thinking on management and leadership.*
>
> - *keep abreast of the latest developments in public governance and management, and act as a repository of best practice.*
>
> - *work closely with research and evaluation units in Departments to develop and strengthen policy evaluation capacity and co-ordinate evaluations of cross-cutting policies.*

14. New institutions and arrangements have been developed to train leaders and staff in the public sector. The Local Government Association has set up the Local Government Improvement and Development Agency, and there will be an equivalent body in Wales; the civil service is setting up a new Centre for Management and Policy Studies, incorporating the Civil Service College; the Department for Education and Employment is setting up the new National College for School Leadership; and the Armed Forces now have a new Joint Services Command and Staff College. They have a vital role to play – working jointly more than they have done in the past – if staff are to be equipped to meet the challenges of delivering the agenda in this White Paper.

15. The civil service is committed to a target that all its organisations become accredited Investors in People by 2000. To date, 40% of civil servants work in such organisations. This is an important element of our commitment to lifelong learning. We must ensure that the civil service meets and exceeds the new National Learning Targets for qualifications.

16. All parts of the public sector have National Training Organisations apart from the civil service. We have applied to establish a Central Government National Training Organisation to develop and maintain a corporate strategy for training and development.

Motivating and involving staff

17. Those who have experience of implementing policies have much to contribute to policy making. This is both motivating for staff and valuable in formulating deliverable policies. We want staff at all levels to contribute to evaluating policies and services, and to put forward ideas about how they might be improved. Ministers have not been surprised to find during workshops and other discussions that front-line staff have many innovative ideas. But, through bureaucracy and an attachment to existing practices for their own sake, we have too often stifled initiative and have discouraged staff from putting ideas forward.

Canterbury City Council – Housing Department.

Hampshire County Council – Basingstoke Information Centre.

The NHS National Taskforce on Staff Involvement:
As part of its commitment to strengthen staff involvement in the NHS, the Government appointed a National Taskforce to look at successful approaches to involving front-line staff in shaping patterns of health care and to make recommendations for action. The 13-strong Taskforce was drawn from a wide cross-section of NHS staff. It includes two nurses, two doctors, a porter, a scientific officer, two managers and an NHS Trust chairman – plus a national trade union officer, an academic and a senior manager from industry. It has consulted widely in the NHS and it has drawn on experience and best practice from both inside and outside the NHS. Its recommendations are now with Ministers and the government response will be published shortly.

18. We have made a start in dismantling these impediments to innovation in our action zones for health, education and employment.

Public sector pay

19. Pay is important to public servants just as it is to other people in society. Public servants must be rewarded fairly for the contribution they make. We must make sure that our approach to pay encourages more of the best people to join and stay.

20. This can be done in a number of ways:

- **Reforming outdated systems.** Inflexible and inefficient practices in pay and conditions must be reformed so that pay can be tailored to the needs of the public service and provide suitable incentives for staff. This means challenging outdated assumptions about public sector pay – for example the idea that 'fair pay' means everybody should get the same increase, or that pay and conditions must all be set nationally.

Modernisation of the NHS pay system:
The Government published its proposals for modernising the NHS pay system in February 1999. We aim to create a pay system which:

- *enables staff to give their best for patients, working in new ways and breaking down traditional barriers.*

- *pays fairly and equitably for work done, with career progression based on responsibility, competence and satisfactory performance.*

- *simplifies and modernises conditions of service, with national core conditions and considerable local flexibility.*

We are making progress on pay reform in various parts of the public sector. Our Green Paper on the teaching profession, *Meeting the Challenge of Change*, set out ambitious proposals for restructuring teachers' pay to improve standards in schools. The Department of Health's recent *Agenda for Change in the NHS* similarly proposed wide-ranging changes to pay designed to improve patient care. These include simplified national pay spines and greater flexibility for local managers to set pay and conditions according to local needs. Local government has reached an agreement on single status pay, paving the way for removing outdated divisions and demarcations between jobs and functions, which delivers local flexibility within a national framework. The Armed Forces will have a new pay system in 2000. And simplified pay and grading structures have been introduced across the civil service. We must build on these developments elsewhere.

- **Recruiting and retaining staff**. Public sector employers must be allowed to recruit, retain and motivate staff with the right skills to do the job. Many parts of the public sector have no difficulty attracting and keeping staff, but there are some areas which do, such as the teaching and nursing professions. The Government is tackling these, both in the pay awards we made earlier this year and through pay reform. We are revising pay scales and introducing new grades – advanced skills teachers and nurse consultants – so that more skilled people can stay in the front line. There may be other areas where we need to pay more to recruit and retain the right staff. These must be carefully identified and clearly targeted.

- **Making best use of non-pay incentives**. Non-pay incentives are often just as important in staff recruitment and motivation as pay. Such incentives may take many forms: better training and development opportunities, good career prospects, opportunities for career breaks, improved working environment, flexible working, family-friendly working practices, recognition in the form of national awards and honours or local workplace schemes. We need to ensure that these are used effectively to attract and reward staff.

- **Rewarding results and performance**. A person's pay should reflect their output, results and performance. This means the best performers – both individuals and teams – and those who contribute most, should be best rewarded. We should challenge systems which give automatic pay increases to poor or inefficient performers. This is why the teaching Green Papers have proposed new performance management arrangements for teachers, movement along pay scales linked to performance, and a new performance threshold giving access to higher pay in cases of high and sustained levels of achievement.

21. The Government is reviewing the way delegated pay and grading systems operate in the civil service. It is clear that performance management is not effective enough. The links between pay and objectives are not always clear. We must use our pay systems – and performance pay in particular – in creative ways to provide effective incentives to achieve sustained high quality performance and to encourage innovation and team-working.

Diversity

22. The public service has a strong tradition of fairness. It is committed to achieving equality of opportunity. But we must accelerate progress on diversity if this country is to get the public service it needs for the new millennium.

23. The public service must be a part of, and not apart from, the society it serves. It should reflect the full diversity of society. At present it does not. Women, people from ethnic minority groups and people with disabilities are seriously under-represented in the more senior parts of the public service.

24. Addressing this is a top priority. The Government wants a public service which values the differences that people bring to it. It must not only reflect the full diversity of society but also be strengthened by that diversity.

25. We have recently launched, with the civil service trade unions, a Joint Charter to address under-representation of ethnic minorities at senior levels. We are also setting targets for women, ethnic minorities and people with disabilities in the senior civil service. And we are requiring Departments to set targets at levels below this.

26. The Government is determined to address the current inequalities in all public services. We must ensure that all public servants and all those we would like to come and work in the public service are treated fairly. They must believe that, irrespective of their backgrounds, they will have a full opportunity to contribute, thrive and progress on the basis of what they bring, the potential they show, and most importantly, what they achieve.

27. Tackling under-representation alone is not enough. A truly effective diverse organisation is one in which the differences individuals bring are valued and used. Currently, we tend to minimise differences and to expect everyone to fit into established ways of working. We should not expect them to. We should be flexible to allow everyone to make the best contribution they can. This has to be reflected in our ways of working, our personnel practices, the way managers manage.

28. There has to be a change of culture. This needs to be led from the top and driven throughout the organisation. The Home Office, the Inland Revenue and Customs & Excise are conducting pilot exercises into how to change culture in this way. We will ensure that the lessons are applied throughout the civil service.

Family-friendly employer

29. The consultation paper on the family *Supporting Families* included our proposals to work closely with employers and other organisations on an awareness and promotional campaign on family-friendly employment practices. The Government itself is determined to be a family-friendly employer. The civil service has a good record, but we can do still better.

Public appointments

30. More than 100,000 people participate in public life through service on the boards of NHS Trusts and advisory and executive bodies. Thousands more act as school governors, magistrates and in a range of other local roles. Involvement in public bodies provides accountability, a wider range of expertise, and allows individuals themselves to play an important and constructive part in local communities. All public appointments should be made on merit.

31. The Government will improve access to public appointments. We are committed to ensuring that public appointments are open to a wide field of candidates so we can draw on the widest possible range of expertise and backgrounds. Potential candidates must be given the opportunity to register an interest and to apply for any vacancies.

32. The Government is committed in principle to equal representation of women and men in public appointments, and pro rata representation of members of ethnic minority groups, on the basis of merit. Last year, according to the independent Commissioner for Public Appointments, women made up 39% of ministerial public appointments and members of ethnic minority groups 7.1%.

Future action

33. To drive forward its vision of how the public service should be equipped for the future, the Government will:

- take forward the debate started by the Prime Minister into how we can equip the public service for the 21st century. The debate must continue to address our approach to public sector pay and conditions of service - how we can best provide flexibility for employers to match pay to the needs of the organisation and to recruit the staff they need, linking pay to outcomes and achievement, rewarding excellence, eliminating inefficiencies, and combining these practices with a creative approach to financial and non-pay incentives.

- publish each year departmental action plans setting out how our commitment in principle to equal representation of women and men in public appointments, and pro rata representation of members of ethnic minority groups, will be delivered in practice.

34. The Government will also drive forward its commitment to involving and motivating staff by setting up 'Learning Labs' at local level as well as nationally. Public servants often know how to overcome problems and inefficiencies, but are held back by red tape and established procedure. Our new scheme will encourage the public sector to test new ways of working by suspending rules that stifle innovation. It will encourage public servants to take risks which, if successful, will make a difference. It will also ensure that successful innovations can be spread around the public service.

35. The Government will take action to strengthen its capacity at the centre to identify and bring into public appointments people of talent and experience.

36. The Government will take the following steps to develop a civil service for the 21st century:

- We will bring more people into the civil service from outside. We will hold more open recruitment competitions for people at various career stages. We will make greater use of short-term contracts. We will increase secondments to and from the rest of the public sector, the voluntary sector and the private sector.

- We will make sure that the commitments to mobility between Departments are delivered. We will identify and remove the barriers to mobility and Departments will be required to set targets, not just for the senior sivil service, as now, but also for staff at more junior levels.

- We will review our recruitment criteria to reflect current and future needs more closely. We will make it easier for people who want to join the civil service to find out about opportunities and to apply for them.

- We will create opportunities for able, younger staff to be promoted to senior positions more quickly. We will seek to increase participation in existing staff development schemes such as the in-service Fast Stream Development Programme and departmental schemes for under-represented groups. We will develop a new scheme for those who show the most potential for early promotion. This will offer both training and experience in a range of jobs across the service and in the wider public sector and outside government.

- We will ensure that personnel systems provide incentives for innovation, collaborative working and excellent service delivery.

- We will make performance pay systems effective both as a reward for high-quality delivery and as an incentive to change behaviour. We will foster innovation and continuous improvement of services in the public sector by rewarding staff who suggest ideas that lead to savings or better services. Government Departments and agencies will introduce schemes which reward staff with a sliding scale percentage of any savings or improvements made as a result of their suggestions.

- We will create positive incentives for success at organisational level too. So we will look for new ways of rewarding organisation performance and success-sharing, for example by using team bonuses or by linking pay, bonuses or other rewards to the achievement of performance or efficiency improvements.

- We will set targets to eliminate the under-representation of groups such as women, ethnic minorities and people with disabilities and change the culture so as to tackle inequality.

- We will train staff in new ways of working and equip them with the skills to meet changing demands.

37. The Government will publish a substantial progress report in the autumn on modernising the civil service.

38. If staff at all levels across the public service are to work more closely together, we must ensure that their institutions facilitate greater interchange, closer co-operation on delivery and joint learning. We will achieve this in two ways:

- The institutions and arrangements for training staff, e.g. the Local Government Improvement and Development Agency, the Centre for Management and Policy Studies and the National College for School Leadership, must work together to share best practice across all the public sector and to learn from each other.

- We will set up, before the summer, a Public Sector Employment Forum bringing together key players from the NHS, education, local government, the civil service and other public sector bodies to exchange experience and work together on issues like career management, identifying potential, performance management, joint training, joint graduate development and joint activity in the recruitment market.

39. We will continue to work closely with the public sector trade unions to achieve our shared goals of committed, fair, efficient and effective public services.

40. All this requires strong leadership from the top and from all public service managers. In the civil service we will ensure that Permanent Secretaries and Heads of Department have personal objectives, on which their performance will be assessed, for taking forward the Government's modernisation agenda and ensuring delivery of the Government's key targets.

Conclusion

1. This White Paper sets out a long-term programme of change – change in the way government makes policy, in the way services are delivered, in the way government uses technology and in the way the public service is valued. It will involve everyone working in the public services, and everyone who uses public services.

2. In the period ahead, the Government will set milestones to chart our course and success criteria so that the users of public services can judge whether the modernisation programme is working. We will report annually on progress.

3. The White Paper was prepared after discussions with many people in the public service and outside. Carrying on this debate is part of taking forward this work. Comments on the modernising programme can be sent in writing to the

Modernising Government Secretariat

Cabinet Office

Horse Guards Road

LONDON SW1P 3AL

or by e-mail to Moderngov@gtnet.gov.uk

Appendix

Websites Links

You can find out more about some of the initiatives mentioned in the White Paper on the following websites:

Page 17:

Comprehensive Spending Review White Paper
http://www.hm-treasury.gov.uk/pub/html/csr/index.html
Sure Start *http://www.dfee.gov.uk*

Page 18:

Social Exclusion Unit *http://www.cabinet-office.gov.uk/seu*
Women's Unit *http://www.cabinet-office.gov.uk/womens-unit*
Crime reduction strategy *http://www.homeoffice.gov.uk/crimprev/cpa.htm*

Page 19:

UK Foresight Programme *http://www.foresight.gov.uk*
Policy Appraisal for Equal Treatment
http://www.cabinet-office.gov.uk/womens-unit/1999/equal.htm
Excellence in Schools *http:// www.dfee.gov.uk*

Page 25:

People's Panel findings *http://www.cabinet-office.gov.uk/servicefirst/index/pphome.htm*

Page 26:

Better Government for Older People Programme
http://www.cabinet-office.gov.uk/servicefirst/index/opmenu.htm

Page 27:

Race relations/Race Relations Forum *http://www.homeoffice.gov.uk/reu/reu.htm*

Page 28:

New Deal for Disabled People *http://www.disability.gov.uk*
and *http://www.dss.gov.uk/hq/press/press798/206.htm*
Access Business *http://www.cabinet-office.gov.uk/bru*

Page 29:

Service First *http://www.cabinet-office.gov.uk/servicefirst*
Employment Service Direct *http://www.employmentservice.gov.uk*
New Commitment to Regeneration *http://www.lga.gov.uk*

Page 30:

Education Action Zones *http://www.dfee.gov.uk*
Public Record Office Family Records Centre *http://www.pro.gov.uk*

Page 31:

Lewisham/Camden One-Stop Shop *http://www.dss.gov.uk/cgis/ndlp/index.htm*
Veterans' Advice Unit *http://www.mod.uk*

Page 32:

Single Work-Focused Gateway *http://www.dss.gov.uk/hq/pubs/gateway/main/sum.htm*
Community Planning *http://www.lga.gov.uk*

Page 36:

Comprehensive Spending Review White Paper
http://www.hm-treasury.gov.uk/pub/htm/csr/index.html
Public Service Agreements White Paper *http://www.hm-treasury.gov.uk*

Page 37:

Public Audit Forum *http://www.public-audit-forum.gov.uk*

Page 38:

Consultation on reform of Deregulation and Contracting Out Act 1994
http://www.cabinet-office.gov.uk/bru/1999/contract.pdf

Page 39:

Public Sector Benchmarking Project *http://www.cabinet-office.gov.uk/eeg*

Page 41:

Best Value *http://www.local-regions.detr.gov.uk*
Better Quality Services *http://www.cabinet-office.gov.uk/eeg/1998/quality/qualmenu.htm*

Page 42:

Charter Mark *http://www.servicefirst.gov.uk*
Land Registry *http://www.landreg.gov.uk*

Page 45:

Our Information Age White Paper *http://www.number-10.gov.uk*
Our Competitive Future White Paper *http://www.dti.gov.uk/cii/elec/elec_com.html*

Page 46:

Brixton Online *http://www.brixton.co.uk*

Page 47:

Consultation Paper on e-commerce *http//www.dti.gov.uk/cii/elec/elec_com.html*
Electronic filing of tax returns *http://www.inlandrevenue.gov.uk/forms_public/index.htm*

Page 48:

NHS Direct *http://www.doh.gov.uk/nhsexec/direct.htm*
National Grid for Learning *http://www.ngfl.gov.uk*
University for Industry *http://www.dfee.gov.uk*

Page 49:

ACCORD *http://www.dss.gov.uk/itsa/index.htm*
Information Age Services for Post Office customers *http://www.royalmail.co.uk*
Public Record Office *http://www.pro.gov.uk*
Modernising Local Government White Paper
http://www.local-regions.detr.gov.uk/lgwp/index.htm
Central IT Unit *http://www.citu.gov.uk*
Cambridge Online *http://www.cam.net.uk*

Page 56:

PM's Charter Mark speech
http://www.cabinet-office.gov.uk/servicefirst/1999/mark/pmspeech.htm

Page 58:

NHS National Taskforce on Staff Involvement
http://www.doh.gov.uk/nhsexec/staffinv.htm

Green Paper *Meeting the Challenge of Change http://www.dfee.gov.uk*

Agenda for Change *http://www.doh.gov.uk/nhsexec/agenda.htm*

Armed Forces pay 2000: *http://www.mod.uk*

Page 59:

Joint Charter with Trades Unions on under-representation of ethnic minorities
http://www.cabinet-office.gov.uk/civilservice/1999/diversity/30-99.htm

Page 60:

Public Appointments/ Commissioner for Public Appointments
http://www.open.gov.uk/ocpa/ocpahome.htm

Page 61:

Fast Stream Development Programme *http://www.cabinet-office.gov.uk/fsesd*

Other useful websites:

No 10 Downing Street: *http://www.number-10.gov.uk*

Cabinet Office: *http://www.cabinet-office.gov.uk*

Welsh devolution: *http://www.wales.gov.uk*

Scottish devolution: *http://www.scottish-devolution.org.uk*

Public Appointments Unit: *http://www.open.gov.uk/pau/pauhome.htm*

Public Bodies 1998: *http://www.official-documents.co.uk/document/caboff/pb98/pb98.htm*

Public Library IT Network: *http://www.lic.gov.uk*

Audit Commission: *http://www.audit-commission.gov.uk*

Printed in the UK for The Stationery Office Limited on behalf of the
Controller of Her Majesty's Stationery Office
Dd 5068772 4/99 077569 Job No. J0078584
Reprinted 1999 with corrections